The Whizzkid's Handbook 2

Peter Eldin

The Whizzkid's Handbook 2

with drawings by Roger Smith

An Armada Original

The Whizzkid's Handbook 2 was first published in
Armada in 1982 by Fontana Paperbacks,
14 St. James's Place, London SW1A 1PS.

Printed in Great Britain by Love & Malcomson Ltd.,
Brighton Road, Redhill, Surrey.

Contents

Foreword

As there was a Foreword in *The Whizzkid's Handbook* and this is the second *Whizzkid's Handbook*, perhaps this introduction should be called the "Fiveword" not the "Foreword". And that is typical of the high level of corn to which you will be treated in the pages that follow!

When *The Whizzkid's Handbook* was published, teachers and adults went grey overnight. This process went one stage further when the book was converted into a successful television series. Now the grown-ups are likely to find their hair dropping out altogether when they discover that *this* book has been published!

This book is completely new. None of the items from the first book have been reused. By popular request (one postcard, without a stamp, from the north of Scotland) PETER ELDIN has put together another invaluable collection of advice to help Whizzkids through school.

School Song

When the Whizzkids first appeared on British television in 1981, their school song was launched on an unsuspecting world. Here, for the benefit of Whizzkids everywhere, are the words:

Whizzkids are the winners, Whizzkids is our name,
We trample on our teachers until they cry with pain.
We pull their hair and poke a finger in their eye,
Whizzkids are the winners, we never have to try.

Whizzkids are fantastic, Whizzkids are so good,
We receive all the cheers, we are never booed.
Falite et vincetis, our motto is in Latin,
Roughly translated, "cheat and you will win".

Whizzkids are the leaders, Whizzkids are the top,
We never are the losers, we never ever flop.
We bend the rules a little, we always win the fame,
Whizzkids are the winners, winning is our game.

Hooray for the Whizzkids!

Reproduced by permission of Southern Television Ltd

Put Your Teacher in Jail

On a piece of card about five centimetres square, draw a picture of your teacher. On the other side of the card draw a number of iron bars.

Now make a small hole in the centre of the two sides of the card. Tie a short piece of string through each hole. If you now twist the string back and forth between the fingers and thumb of each hand, the card will begin to revolve. When it is going quite fast your teacher will appear to be behind bars. Hooray!

He or she will stay in this jail until you stop twisting the string—or until the teacher catches you!

How to Fool Your Maths Teacher

Divide a piece of paper or card measuring 20 by 20 centimetres into 64 squares as shown. Each division is 2.5 centimetres square. Cut the card into the four pieces indicated by the thick lines.

Show the card to your mathematics teacher with the pieces put together as in the first drawing. Show him or her that there are 64 squares. Now tell your teacher that you are such a mathematical genius that you can increase the area of the card without adding anything to it. Your teacher may well believe that you are a mathematical genius (huh?) but he will not believe you can increase the area of the card.

Now for the surprise. Rearrange the pieces into the shape shown in the second illustration. Your teacher will now have quite a shock, for when he counts the squares he will discover there are now 65! You have created an extra 2.5 square centimetres from absolutely nothing!

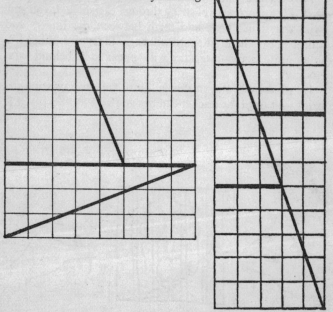

Modern Art

If you want to get good marks from your art teacher and you cannot draw a straight line, the dining-room curtains, or water from a well, try doing some modern art with this little device.

All you need is a piece of card which you cut to any shape you like. Push a drawing pin through the card at any place.

Pin the card to a sheet of paper and then draw around the card. Now move the card slightly and draw around it again. Keep repeating this until you are thoroughly fed up.

You will now have an attractive abstract pattern. If you have sufficient patience you could either use a different coloured pencil each time or colour the pattern after you have finished. You could also try varying the design by using several different shapes in the same pattern.

If you draw the shapes close together you will often find that the finished picture appears to move. This is known as *kinetic art* which, as you probably know, is derived from the Greek word *kinetikos* meaning "putting in motion".

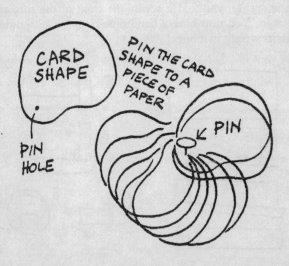

CARD SHAPE

PIN THE CARD SHAPE TO A PIECE OF PAPER

PIN

PIN HOLE

Cash on Hand

When a Whizzkid wants to buy something, he or she simply uses a finger ring for money. Why? Because the ring is made out of money, that's why!

To make a ring from a £5 note, or any other paper money, is really quite simple. This is all you have to do: Place the note down on the table (a new note is best). Fold up the bottom half centimetre. Now fold the top half down and tuck the edge under the first fold. Your note should now look like the third illustration.

Next, fold it in half lengthways. Then take the left end of the note and fold it upwards 90 degrees to form the shape in the fifth illustration. The length of the upright section should be three times the width of the folded note.

Roll the right end of the note back and around to form a ring. You can use your finger to help make the ring the correct size. You should now be in the position shown in the sixth illustration.

Fold the upright section down over the vertical section and then around to the back of the ring. Now take the right-hand vertical section and fold it across the front of the ring and tuck it in. You now have a handsome ring that is certainly worth its weight in money!

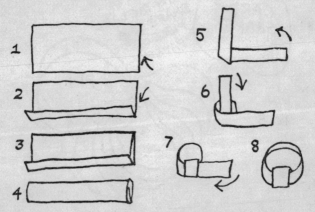

Dining Room Definitions

In the first *Whizzkid's Handbook* it was explained that school dining room supervisors tend to give their meals fancy names. A short dictionary was included giving the school name and the actual name of various meals so that school-children could readily identify what was put before them.

Many Whizzkids sent in other names for school meals, some of which were respectable enough to put into print. So here, for the benefit of Whizzkids everywhere, are some further translations of the names given to school meals.

School Name	Actual Name
Coq au vin	chicken on a lorry
Plums and custard	conkers in slime
Noodle soup	brain juice
Scrambled eggs	stewed brains
Spaghetti bolognaise	swamp-covered shoelaces
Ring doughnuts	pigmy's loo seats
Ravioli	dead teabags
Boiled potatoes	soggy ping-pong balls
Bread rolls	cannonballs
Cabbage	gangrene
Steak and kidney	Kate and Sydney
Rice with jam	septic wound
Shortbread	bits of Stonehenge
Brussel sprouts	mouldy prunes
Gravy	axle grease
Chocolate custard	Thames mud
Cheese	soap
Sausages and mash	suspicion and trash
Lettuce	rabbit food
Egg and chips	eyeballs and fingers
Curry	cook's revenge
Jam tart	blood-soaked bandage
Soup	washing-up water

Excuses for Being Late

If you are ever late for school, it is more than likely that your teacher will demand some explanation (spoil-sport!). If you do not have a reasonable excuse try one of the following:

I broke my ankle (rather a lame excuse).

I squeezed my toothpaste too hard and it took me ages to get it back into the tube.

You rang the bell before I got here.

I must have over-washed.

There was a notice on my bus saying, "Dogs Must Be Carried" and it took me ages to find one.

Last night I dreamt about a football match and it went into extra time, so I stayed asleep to see the finish.

There are only seven people in our house but the alarm clock was set for eight.

There's a sign outside that says "School Ahead — Go Slow", so I obeyed it.

Picture the Word

Can you say what word each of these pictures represents. (Watch out for number six — it's a French word).

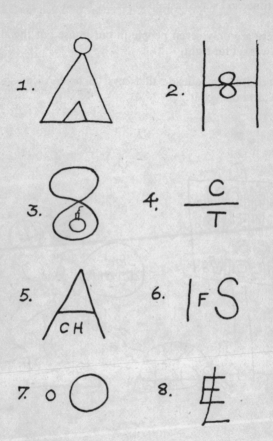

1.

2.

3.

4. C / T

5.

6. IFS

7. o O

8.

Answers on page 126

Bet You Didn't Know

School subjects are sometimes so confusing that it is little wonder that pupils often get mixed up. This confusion leads to mistakes which the pupil is not aware of. Such mistakes are called "howlers" and some of the classic ones have become quite well known. A few of them are listed below:

Water boils at a higher temperature in a Fahrenheit thermometer than in a Centigrade thermometer.

Columbine was the wife of Columbus.

Words in a sloping type are called hysterics.

WOLSEY SAVED HIS LIFE BY DYING BEFORE HE GOT TO LONDON.

If you squeeze the juice out of mud you get dust.

the opposite of evergreen is nevergreen!

A GROUP OF PEOPLE SINGING IS CALLED ACQUIRE

Hard cheese

The Pied Piper promised to rid Hamelin of all its rates.

When a dog has puppies it is called a litre.

Degas was famous for painting ballet dancers and other objects.

In some churches they burn insects

Postcard Puzzler

This is a tricky item to carry around with you. People get most frustrated trying to solve it.

You will need three postcards or pieces of thin card to make the puzzle. Cut the three cards into the shapes shown in the illustrations—an oblong, two triangles joined together, and a ring. Bend the oblong at the centre and place the ring over it as shown in the second illustration. Try not to put a crease in the oblong as that may give your victim some idea as to how to solve the puzzle.

Now fold the two triangles in half. Place them over one of the bars of the folded part of the oblong as shown in the third illustration. Pull the ring along and then down over the upper part of the triangles. Open up the oblong and it will appear as in the fifth illustration.

Give the complete thing to your victim and challenge him to remove the triangles without tearing or cutting any of the shapes. It seems impossible, but all you have to do is the reverse of the moves that put them there in the first place.

A Clean Dirty Prank

If you have smooth-topped tables in your school dining room you can pull this prank to frustrate the cooks.

Fill a glass tumbler to the brim with water. Place a piece of paper or card on top of the glass. The card must be wider than the mouth of the glass. Put one hand flat on the card and now turn the whole lot (glass, water and card) upside down.

Being such a genius, you already know that it is now possible to remove your hand from the card and everything will stay in place. No doubt you also know that this is due to hydrostatic pressure. Clever little monkey, aren't you!

Now place the glass, still upside down, on the table. Hold the glass and very carefully pull the card from beneath it. Some water will seep out at this point but do not worry. If the whole lot seeps out, then you can worry. If all has gone well you are left with a full glass of water upside down on the table!

Now go out of the dining room leaving the booby-trapped glass where it is. Anyone who picks up the glass will get soaked. If a teacher orders you to pick it up, don't worry. Carefully slide the glass to the edge of the table. Move it slightly over the edge so the water pours into another glass held below. It's simple when you know how!

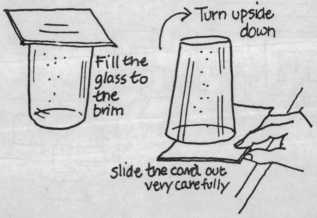

Fill the glass to the brim

Turn upside down

slide the card out very carefully

Write Write Right

A lesson in spelling from that prolific English author, Anon.

Write we know is written right
When we see it written write.
But when we see it written rite
We know it is not written right.
For write to have been written right
Must not be written right nor rite,
Nor yet should it be written wright
But write—
for that's the way it's written right!

23

Shadow Zoo

Although they are fairly easy to do, shadow pictures always seem to impress people. Because of this, every Whizzkid should have a few of them in his or her repertoire.

Apart from a strong light source such as the school projector, all you need is a pair of hands. So, go and find your hands. If you cannot find them, here is a clue: They are the grubby things at the end of each arm. You can now try the figures shown on the following pages.

FLYING DOVE
One of the easiest shadow pictures to form is the flying dove. To make this, simply hold your hands in the position shown and the dove will be formed. How do you make it fly? That, too, is simple. All you have to do is keep your fingers together and move them up and down in imitation of flapping wings.

SPRUCE GOOSE
This is another bird that can be formed very easily. To get a more realistic effect, roll your sleeve up first. By opening and closing your third and little fingers you can make the goose open and close its beak.

24

SWAN SONG

This swan can be made even more effective if you make him shake his tail. You will find that you can also turn the head and neck around to make it look as if the bird is cleaning its feathers.

FUNNY BUNNY

Hold your hands as shown and the shadow formed will be that of a cute little bunny rabbit. Aah! By moving the top two fingers you can make the rabbit's ears wiggle. If you close the left hand slightly you can make him blink. By moving the second, third, and little fingers of the left hand you can produce a realistic twitching of the nose and mouth.

TRUNK CALL

Another easy shadow to form is that of an elephant. Swing the trunk to and fro to make it more effective. With practice you will be able to move the fingers slightly to reveal the elephant's eye.

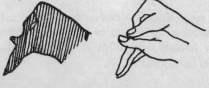

BULLY BEEF

The next picture shows how to form the shape of a bull. Place a small ring between your fingers and it will look as if the bull has a ring in its nose.

PARROT PERCH

The secret of making this parrot move realistically is to remember that if you move the body you must also move the tail at the same time.

CUTE CAT

For the shadow of a cat you will have to be wearing a coat, for this will form the animal's body. The right hand makes the head and one finger of the left hand makes a wiggling tail.

To make your shadow demonstrations more fun, you could try imitating the creatures you are showing. It can provide your friends with a bit of a laugh and makes a welcome relief from lessons.

Facts to Bamboozle Teachers

Teachers are always impressed when you tell them something they do not know (for, whatever they say, they do not know everything.) Here are some true facts with which you can bamboozle your teachers. Learn some of them and use them in your next essay. They should help you to get a better mark.

To make just one spoonful of honey, bees have to visit some 5,000 flowers.

About 400 newspapers can be made from the wood pulp of one tree.

A housewife walks an average of eight miles a day to do her housework.

The digestive juices from the stomach of a shark are so strong they can burn a man's skin.

It is impossible to fold a piece of paper in half more than seven times.

Horses used for riding in Bavaria have to wear number plates.

Contrary to popular opinion, bulls do not respond to the colour red. They are colour blind.

You are not allowed to send red packets or envelopes through the post in the British Isles. The same is also true of any other colour likely to cause strain on the eyes of Post Office staff.

Cut Some Work Out of Homework

Teachers love giving kids homework—it stops them doing the things they enjoy. But homework need not be quite such a chore if you approach it correctly. Try the following tips and you will find it easier to do your homework—who knows, you may even come to enjoy it!

1. One of the secrets of doing homework effectively is advance planning. Try to draw up a timetable for each evening's work. On this timetable write down the times you expect to start and finish each piece of work.

As a general rule, watching television is banned, but that does not mean that you should miss your favourite programme. Plan your timetable around it. Provided that you do not end up spending more time viewing than working, this should work out quite well.

2. Mix the subjects you have to study on any one evening. If you stick to just the one subject all the time your brain will soon become tired and you will get bored. Vary the subjects and the work becomes easier and more interesting.

28

Ideal homework conditions

3. It is a good idea to do your homework in the same place every time. As far as possible this should be a well-lit, well-ventilated room without any tempting distractions. You will need a desk or table on which to work (see page 46) and an upright chair.

4. When doing homework have plenty of short rest periods. There is a limit to how much concentrated work you can do. If you try to go on for too long you will actually achieve less than you could have done in a shorter period. So, after every fifteen minutes of concentrated study, take a two minute break. During this time wander around the room, walk in the back garden, or have a drink. This technique is especially effective when you are trying to learn something. You will find that you can learn and remember material much more effectively if you tackle it in several short learning sessions with suitable breaks rather than one long session with no breaks whatsoever.

5. Make the best use of any reading that you have to do. As this is an important subject it is dealt with separately on the next page.

Read, Learn and Inwardly Digest

"Read, learn and inwardly digest." That's a favourite command of many teachers when dishing out homework. Unfortunately, they never tell you the best way of going about it. And with reading, as with any other activity, there is a right and a wrong way to approach it. To make the best use of any reading you do, whether it be for homework or for your own pleasure, try the following tips:

1. Before starting to read, think about the subject. Try to recall everything you know about it. A good technique for this is to give an imaginary speech on the subject. Give the speech out loud—your teddy bear will find it very interesting.

2. Now read the passage you have to study, but don't read it passively. Think all the time you are reading. Try to compare the new information you are learning with what you know already (which may not be very much). Take your time and question everything. Your reading may take a little longer than usual, but you will gain more from it in the end.

3. Read aloud. As a general rule, teachers discourage reading aloud as it slows up the reading process. But from a learning point of view it is an excellent technique and will help you to remember the material much more easily.

4. Do not just read one book on the subject. Go through as many as you can. You will find some books more useful than others and what may not be explained fully in one could be explained in more detail in another.

5. When you have finished reading do some more thinking. Think about the things you have just learned. Once again, it is a good idea to give an imaginary speech on the subject. This time, instead of boring your teddy bear (who is probably pretending to be asleep anyway), stand in front of a mirror (try not to scream at the ugly sight) and imagine you are a television personality presenting a programme about what you have just read.

Try these tips and you will find that you will remember much more than you did previously, and it might not be long before you are top of the class. Of course, these tips have been given on the assumption that you can read—if you can't, just look at the pictures!

I couldn't bear it any longer

Button Release

Make two short cuts in a postcard as shown. The cuts should be about 5 centimetres long and about 1¼ centimetres apart. Below the cuts make a small hole. Thread a length of cotton through the slits and then through the hole. To each end of the cotton tie a button. You should now have the peculiar-looking article shown in the illustration.

Hand the whole thing to a teacher and challenge him to remove the cotton and the buttons from the card. He is not allowed to cut the cotton or the card in any way.

Before challenging someone else to do it, you had better learn how it is done yourself! All you have to do is to bend the card in half until you can push the cut strip (A) through the hole. Push it right through until there is an appreciable loop of the strip on the other side of the hole. Push one of the buttons through the loop and then return the card to its original position. The cotton and the buttons are now free from the card.

CB Talk

CB language—the words used by owners of Citizens' Band radio—can be very useful to a Whizzkid. It will enable you to talk to other Whizzkids without adults having the slightest clue as to what you are on about. There are a lot of expressions to learn, but here are a few to give you a start:

CB Word	Meaning
Alligator	person with a big mouth
Anklebiter	a naughty child
Blood box	ambulance
Brain bucket	crash helmet
Eyeball	see/look
Gimme five	shake hands
Good buddy	friend
Grandma lane	slow lane

Anklebiter → Alligator →

Hair-cut palace	low bridge
Land line	telephone
Lay an eye on that	take a look at that
Lettuce	paper money
Motion lotion	petrol
Park your mouth	shut up
Roller skate	car
Skin clock	wristwatch
Snore shelf	bed
Snow white and the seven dwarfs	a wedding
Super slab	motorway
10 - 4	okay
10 - 9	please repeat that
Ulcer emporium	restaurant

English Language

One of the compulsory lessons in British schools is English Language. There are some 490,000 words in the English language but the average person uses only about 50,000 of them. Children of school-leaving age use about 5,000 words in speech but up to about 10,000 in written work.

There are even fewer words that can be made from the letters of "English Language". See how many words of four or more letters you can make from "English Language", and compare your score with those shown below and with the list at the back of the book.

. . . .

. . . .

. . . .

. . . .

. . . .

. . . .

. . . .

. . . .

SCORES: 30   good   60   stupendous!

           40   very good   80   you are a genius!

           50   excellent   100   cheat!

Hen Eggs that's two

Answers on page 126

Multi Thread

A great many people have trouble threading a needle. You boast to the needlework teacher that you never have any trouble. "In fact," you say, "I can thread a needle several times quite easily." To prove this claim you take a small box from your pocket. Inside the box is an ordinary needle through the eye of which are a multitude of threads!

This is how you do it: First thread the needle in the normal way. Now push the point of the needle through the thread some fifteen centimetres from the end. Do not open up the strands of the thread too much—just enough to get the needle through.

Now pull the thread down over the eye of the needle and over the thread you originally pushed through it. You should now be in the position shown in the second illustration.

Take the thread at the point marked and pull it down so the loop of thread is pulled through the eye. The separated strands will pull another piece of thread through the eye so you now have two lengths of thread going through it.

Continue pulling until you have as many threads going through the eye as you can manage. Obviously the larger the eye of the needle you use, the easier it is going to be and the more threads you will manage to get through.

With a pair of scissors cut through the bottom of the loops and cut away the piece that passes through itself. You are left with a needle that has been threaded many, many times—and the needlework teacher will never *cotton* on as to how you achieved this amazing feat.

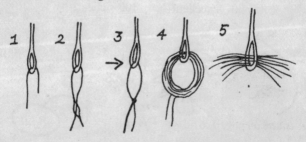

Royalty in Rhyme

How would you like to amaze your history teacher by reciting all of the kings and queens of England in their correct order?

The monarchs are: William I, William II, Henry I, Stephen, Henry II, Richard I, John, Henry III, Edward I, Edward II, Edward III, Richard II, Henry IV, Henry V, Henry VI, Edward IV, Edward V, Richard III, Henry VII, Henry VIII, Edward VI, Mary I, Elizabeth I, James I, Charles I, Charles II, James II, William III, Mary II, Anne, George I, George II, George III, George IV, William IV, Victoria, Edward VII, George V, George VI, Elizabeth II.

To remember that lot would be quite a remarkable feat. But it is not quite so difficult as it appears if you cheat a little—by means of a rhyme. When you have learned the rhyme you will be able to quote the name of every king and queen of England since 1066. That should earn you some good marks in history. So start learning:

Willie, Willie, Harry, Steve.
Harry, Dick, John, Harry Three.
One, two, three Eds, Dicky Two.
Harry Four, Five, Six then who?
Edward Four, Five, Dick the Bad.
Harrys twain and Ed the Lad.
Mary, Lizzie, James the Vain.
Charlie, Charlie, James again.
William and Mary, Anna Gloria.
Four Georges, William, and Victoria.
Edward, George, and George again.
Queen Elizabeth now to reign.

More Bet You Didn't Know

Here are some classic howlers from school exercise books:

England used to be Roman Catholic until Queen Elizabeth I made it Christian.

There are lots of currants in the sea.

A trade union is a place you go to when you lose your job.

Heat moves through water by conviction.

The Armada had to wait until Drake finished his game of bowels.

The four seasons are salt, mustard, vinegar, pepper

The cuckoo lays other birds' eggs in its nest.

Tadpoles eat one another until they become frogs.

Parallel lines never meet unless you bend them.

To remove air from a flask, fill it with water. Tip the water out and put the cork in quick.

A posthumous work is something written to someone after they are dead.

The Gorgons had long snakes in their hair. They look like women only more horrible.

Whizzkid's Giant Crossword

Watch out! Many of the clues to this crossword are cryptic. This means that the clue is not so straightforward as it may sound and that it holds a secret clue to the answer. For example, words like "rearranged" or "upset" in a cryptic clue often indicate an anagram to be solved. Just think about this clue for a moment: *Performing place in a jumbled tree hat*. (7) Here the word "jumbled" could suggest an anagram—perhaps of the words "tree hat" as they contain the seven letters required. The other clue is "performing place". Try to make a "performing place" from "tree hat" and you end up with "theatre" which is the correct answer!

Cryptic clues can work in several different ways. Sometimes they can be asking you to add or take away letters from a particular word to find the answer. Words like "remove" or "take" in a clue might indicate this. Here is an example: *Remove a drinking vessel to find this piece of wood.* (5) Another word for a "drinking vessel" is "cup". If you think of longer words that contain the letters CUP you might come up with "cupboard". If you take "cup" from "cupboard" you are left with "board"—another name for a "piece of wood"!

Not all the clues in this crossword are cryptic, but there are some—so keep your wits about you as you try to solve them.

Across

1. Make the cat here take the lesson. (7)
5. Hungarian inventor of a puzzling cube. (5)
7. The definite article. (3)
10. Clever thought. (4)
12. Upset heat dreams for the top man at school. (10)
18. A preposition. (2)
20. Drink made with honey. (4)
21. Remove a tack from a physical assault to get this preposition. (2)
22. English, arithmetic and geography are some of these at school. (7)
25. Rearranged rats top the bill. (4)
27. Short operation. (2)
28. Part of a curved line. (3)
29. Large vessel for brewing tea. (3)
30. A laugh in short. (2)
32. One in the grass? (5)
35. It's said Whizzkids hate washing with this. It's a lye. (4)
37. If I am, he . . . (2)
38. A male teacher is one. (3)
40. Gold. (2)
41. Popular name for a lion. (3)
42. . . . de Janeiro, main port of Brazil. (3)
44. Language of the ancient Romans. (5)
46. A type of mathematics. (7)
48. Midday is the same both ways. (4)
51. Fee, . . ., Fo, Fum, (said the giant). (2)
52. On the way. (5)
55. Before Christ, initially. (2)
57. French petrol. (7)

59. Musical note but it sounds like bread mixture. (3)
60. Room at the top of a house. (5)
62. It's in a tree, you fool! (3)
64. Expression of surprise sounds like the centre of an apple. (3)
65. It's performed by a magician. (5)
67. French thou. (2)
68. To interlock wool to make clothes. (4)
70. A mathematical symbol. (2)
72. It goes with neither. (3)
74. The act of using your brain. (8)
78. Remnant of cloth. (3)
79. It's backwards for 51 across. (2)
80. Spanish the. (2)
81. Initially it's in the afternoon. (2)
83. School for hospital staff? (7)
84. Snake that is said to have killed Cleopatra. (3)

Down

1. Prefix for three. (3)
2. Sounds like eight, have eaten. (3)
3. Absolute confusion. (5)
4. Third person masculine. (2)
6. Form of school transport. (3)
8. It holds back water. (3)
9. Mister in short. (2)
11. Antlered animal. (4)
13. Short Desmond. (3)
14. School subject concerning numbers. (11)
15. Girl's name the same both ways. (3)
16. Little thanks. (2)
17. Famous school of note. (4)
19. Enemy. (3)
22. Short room for experiments. (3)
23. A gathering of fish or pupils. (6)
24. Junior's opposite. (6)
26. An athletic pursuit. (7)
31. Initially the Automobile Association. (2)
33. For this adverb remove a cent from climbing. (2)
34. *Francais* in english. (6)
35. Around the world it can be Black, Yellow, or Red but it is still greeny-blue. (3)
36. Senior pupil with some authority but not quite perfect. (7)
39. Preposition for time when. (2)
43. Sacred wading bird of ancient Egypt. (4)
45. Reply in the negative. (2)
47. What you do as you get older. (3)
49. Woodwind instrument. (4)

50. Sounds crazy to be pulled at Christmas. (8)
53. Not off. (2)
54. A net that is tidy. (4)
56. Puppeteers have pull with these. (7)
58. Article of girl's clothing. (5)
61. There are twenty hundredweights in one. (3)
63. One in the eye for a scholar. (5)
66. Cutting instrument. (5)
69. Today without the day. (2)
71. Not out. (2)
73. Move yourself fast. (3)
74. It belongs to him if it this. (3)
76. You will open the lock with it. (3)
77. Talk a lot about hydrogen? (3)
82. A short member of Parliament. (2)

Answers on page 126

43

Candid Camera

With this neat little device you can pretend to take instant photographs of your teachers and friends. All you need is some paper, a sharp pencil and a pair of scissors.

Take a piece of paper measuring about 10 by 20 centimetres and fold it in half. Draw a square on the front of the paper. In the centre of the square draw a funny face.

Push the point of the pencil into each corner of the square to make four holes through both pieces of paper. Open up the paper and use the four holes as a guide to draw another square on the lower sheet. In this square draw the front of the camera.

Cut down each side of both squares from the top holes to the bottom holes. On the lower sheet cut across the top of the square. Cut across the bottom of the square on the top sheet. You now have a sort of flap on each sheet. Now close the folded paper and tuck the two flaps together.

The paper should now have the camera showing to the front. Show the camera to your subject explaining that it is the latest instant camera. Offer to take the subject's portrait. Now all you have to do to develop the picture is to open and close the paper. This makes the picture come into view. If the picture is a funny one you had better get ready to run for your life!

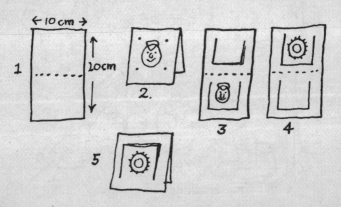

From Last to First

If any of your friends come last in a test, a sporting event, or an exam, tell them you can change last into first. When they challenge you to do so, show them the four letters L A S T cut from cardboard. The letter L must be like the one shown in the picture.

Place the letters on a table and ask your friends if they can change last into first. To do this they must not add any letters and they are not allowed to mutilate the letters in any way.

When your mates have tried and failed, you simply remove the letter A and move the L alongside ST. The L can now be read as the number 1, and so the three letters form 1st—and you have changed last into first, just as you promised.

simply amazing!!!

45

Desk for Homework

Homework is one of the many things that teachers have devised to upset pupils. But it does not deter Whizzkids for they follow the tips given on page 28.

To make homework a little less of a chore, you will need a homework desk. If you haven't got a suitable piece of furniture you can make this simple desk. All you need is a large sheet of hardboard. Its exact measurements will depend upon the space you have available but about 1 by .5 metres should be sufficient.

This desk top is supported by two wooden crates. With their open sides to the front, the crates will serve as a useful place to put books and papers. The desk will be quite adequate as it is, but you could cover it with a cloth or some sticky-backed plastic if you wish.

Barmy Barometer

If you ever study the weather in your science lessons at school, you will find this barometer very useful. There is nothing to make and yet the barometer will prove an extremely accurate weather reporter.

All you have to do is take a piece of paper and screw it up into a ball. Just before you go to bed, open the window and place the paper ball outside on the windowsill. In the morning take a look at your paper ball. If the paper is wet then it has been, or still is, raining. If the paper is dry then it is a fine morning. And if the paper has disappeared, it is windy!

On the Top

Place a cup upside down on the table. Alongside it put three dead matches. Now challenge your victim to put one match on top of the cup using only the other two matches.

Your friend will, with a bit of practice, manage to lift up one match between the other two and deposit it on the cup. He will be very pleased with his success—until you point out that he has not put the match on the top of the cup as you said. He has put it on the bottom!

The Long Walk

Next time you are in the school playground or on the playing field, try this joke on one of your more gullible friends.

You tell your friend that you are a great fortune-teller. Say that you have discovered a way of predicting the future by looking at a person's shoe. It may take all of your persuasive powers, but eventually your friend will give in and offer one of his shoes to test your amazing ability to predict the future.

Trying not to pull a face because it smells so much of his stinky feet, you now gaze intently into the shoe. You then solemnly pronounce your prediction: "I predict that you are going to take a long walk." Then you throw his shoe as far away as you can. To recover his shoe, he will have to take a long walk—just as you predicted!

Groans in Geography

Why is a stupid boy like the Amazon jungle?
They are both dense.

Where is Liverpool?
Top of the First Division.

What Scottish island do you
have to look up to?
Skye.

What is the climate of New
Zealand like?
*It must be cold, for the meat they send to
Britain is always frozen.*

Which is furthest away—America
or the Moon?
*It must be America for you can see
the Moon.*

What are the chief minerals
to be found in Italy?
Orangeade and lemonade.

What is the coldest country in the world?
Chile.

Where are the Andes?
At the end of the armies.

What do we get from Germany
Germs.

Where is the Sahara Desert?
You're the geography master—you tell me.

What is the laziest mountain in the world?
Everest.

What is the world's slipperiest country?
Greece.

What country is ravenous?
Hungary.

What do you know about the Dead Sea?
I didn't even know it was ill.

Whizzkid's Library

Here are some of the most popular books to be found on the shelves (and on the floor) in the Whizzkid's school library:

Francis Neer

Juliet Thelott

WHY DID I DO THAT? by Ada Reason
SEASONAL CELEBRATIONS by Chris Mass
BRIGHT BEAM by Ray Ovlite
ACROSS THE CHANNEL by Francis Neer
HARD PUZZLE by Sarah Waytodoit
YOU'VE GOT LOTS by Len Meesum
GAP IN THE MOUNTAINS by Val Lee
NAUGHTY BOY by Willie B. Goode
EMPTY PLATES by Juliet Thelott
THE BREAKFAST by Hammond Ex
TALL TREE by Douglas Fir
RING OF FIRE by Catherine Weel
SNOW FALL by Ava Lanche
THERE AND BACK by Carmen Engowin
DID HE DO IT? by Betty Didunt

DID HE DO IT?

Betty Didunt

So You Think You Know Everything

Think you know everything? Think you are such a brain box that you are a walking encyclopedia? Then try this simple general knowledge quiz. Some of the answers may not be quite as simple as you think! But, no cheating now. Don't look at the answers in the back of the book until you have tried each question.

1. What cheese is made backwards?
2. How did the Druids build Stonehenge?
3. Why do church bells ring on Sundays?
4. How do you make a radio?
5. How much earth is there in a hole 10 centimetres square by 10 centimetres deep?
6. What can you hold without touching it?
7. What was the Prime Minister's name in 1975?
8. What question can never be answered truthfully with "yes"?
9 What lies at the bottom of the ocean and shakes?
10. What is raspberry-flavoured, lies at the bottom of the ocean and shakes?

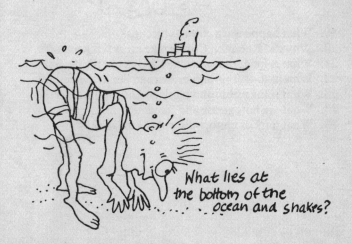

What lies at the bottom of the ocean and shakes?

11. What did the scarf say to the hat?
12. What occurs once in a minute, twice in a moment, but never in a hundred years?
13. Why is the letter T like an island?
14. What does a nuclear scientist have for his tea?
15. What did the Spaniard say to his chickens?
16. What goes ninety-nine, bonk, ninety-nine, bonk, ninety-nine, bonk?
17. If you have umpires in cricket, and referees in football, what do you have in bowls?
18. Why are elephants wrinkled?

Why are elephants wrinkled?

19. What happens if a cow has hiccups?
20. Why did Robinson Crusoe take every weekend off?
21. What is long, thin and white and lies in the desert?
22. What is long, thin and brown and lies in the desert?
23. What is long, thin and black and lies in the desert?
24. What are hot, greasy and romantic?
25. What famous chiropodist ruled England?

Answers on page 126

Artful Art

Here are some crafty drawings you can show your art teacher and your friends. Draw one of the pictures and then ask people to guess what it is. When you have used all these and the ones shown on page 106, try making up some of your own. If you cannot guess what each picture represents, you will find the answers at the back of the book.

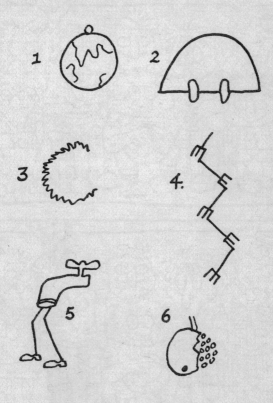

Answers on page 127

Changing-Room Changes

These two pictures show members of the football team of Strange Hill School in the changing-rooms prior to a match. At first sight the pictures look identical, but there are ten subtle differences between the two. Can you spot them?

Answers on page 127

Soggy Semolina

This is a little ditty about school dinners that is popular throughout the British Isles (the ditty not the dinners). It is sung to the traditional tune of *Frère Jacques*.

COLD POTATOES
COLD POTATOES
ROTTEN PEAS
ROTTEN PEAS
SOGGY SEMOLINA
SOGGY SEMOLINA
WATER QUICK
I FEEL SICK

Arithmetic Exam

Test your arithmetical (that's a long word) ability with this mathematical (another long word) examination.

1. Write down eight eights in such a way that they add up to one thousand.

2. Write down the number eleven thousand eleven hundred and eleven.

3. If a postcard and a stamp cost 25p, and the stamp costs 20p more than the postcard, what is the cost of the postcard?

4. Which is heavier, a pound of feathers or a pound of lead?

5. Which is the greater—six dozen dozen or half a dozen dozen?

6. A brick weighs 14 kilograms and half a brick. How much does a brick and a half weigh?

7. In your head multiply 1,639,344,262,295,081,967, 213,114,754,098,360,655,737,704,918,032,787 by 71.

Answers on page 127

Fly Me

Every Whizzkid should know how to make a paper aeroplane. It's a very useful way of sending messages across the classroom when the teacher is asleep.

There are many different ways of making paper aeroplanes, but this one is probably the simplest. All you need is a sheet of A4 paper (210 x 297 millimetres). Fold the paper in half lengthways. Turn the top two corners down to meet the centre fold. Now take the point marked X and fold it down to the central crease. Do exactly the same on the other side.

The next thing to do is to fold each wing in half so that its straight edge meets the centre fold as shown in the fourth drawing. Press all the creases down firmly.

To make your aeroplane fly, hold the centre fold between the thumb and forefinger of one hand. Now move them upwards to open out the wing formed by the last fold you made. It is a good idea to put a strip of sticky tape along the plane's undercarriage to give it a bit of weight and to prevent the folds from opening, but this is not absolutely necessary.

Throw the plane into the air (remember to leave go or you may launch yourself as well) and you have lift off.

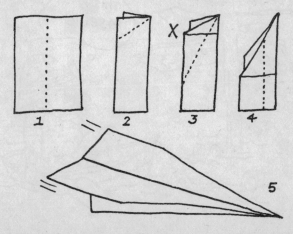

River Arrangement

The names listed below are of famous rivers in many parts of
the world. Using skill, judgement, logic, or plain guesswork
see if you can fit all the names into the grid shown opposite.

ALTMAHA
AMAZON
AMUR
BARROW
COLORADO
COLOMBIA
DARLING
DANUBE
EUPHRATES
GARONNE

LENA
LOIRE
MURRAY
ORINOCO
OTTAWA
RHINE
RHONE
SEINE
THAMES
URAL

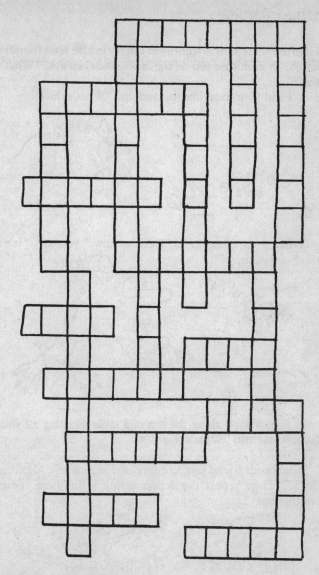

Answers on page 127

What's This

Here are some simple stunts you can try to give your friends a laugh. In each case you do the action and then ask, "What's this?"

1. Hold your hand like this and say, "What's this?"

When your friend says, "I don't know," you say, "It's a dead one of these."

2. Run a hand along the top of a table wiggling all your fingers and ask, "What's this?"

When your friend says he doesn't know, you say, "Neither do I." Then repeat the action saying, "But here comes another one."

2.

What's this?

I don't know, but here comes another one".

3. Hold both arms outstretched and flap your hands up and down like the wings of a bird. Ask your friends what it is and when they give up, say: "It's a man painting both sides of a school corridor at the same time."

4. Close one eye.
"What's this?"

A man who took two
sleeping pills but only one
of them worked.

4. What's this?

5. Put the tips of the fingers of both
hands together. Open and close the hands a few times, keeping the fingers touching. "What's this?"

5.

What's
this?

A spider doing press-ups on a mirror.

6. Hold both hands out in front of you and move the fingers up and down. "What's this?"

6.

A schoolboy washing his socks and shooing the flies away!

How to Be Top in Art

You do not have to be an artistic genius to come top in art, for some drawing is really quite simple. Try the pictures shown on the pages that follow.

Baby Pin-up
Draw a safety pin as shown. You can now change the picture into that of a baby just by the addition of a few simple strokes.

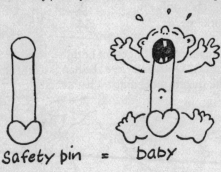

Safety pin = baby

You Are a Clown
Say to your art teacher: "I can turn you into a clown." Write down the word YOU as shown below. It is now a simple matter to change the letters into the face of a clown.

you ave a clown

Early to Rise

Draw a small hill and the sun as shown. Tell your art teacher it is a picture of you getting up in the morning. Your teacher will not be able to see the connection, whereupon you say, "Actually that is the sun rising in the morning." You then add a few lines to the first drawing to form the second picture as you say, "And this is me rising in the morning."

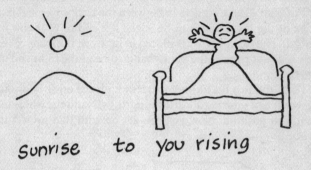

Sunrise to you rising

Ghost Mountain

Draw the squiggle shown below. Tell your teacher it is a picture of Ghost Mountain. No doubt your teacher will be extremely impressed by your amazing artistic ability! He or she will be even more impressed when you add a few more squiggles to produce the ghost of Ghost Mountain!

GHOST MOUNTAIN TO "GHOST OF THE MOUNTAIN"

Make a Desk Book Rack

It is quite possible that you will need to keep some reference books on your homework desk, or at least near to hand. To stop them from falling over just when you are writing up an important project, you can make these simple book supports.

All you need is a cardboard box—the stronger the better. Cut the corners from the box as shown in the illustration.

Put one of these corners in between the back cover and last page of the book that is to be at the left end of your row of books. The other corner is placed in between the front cover and the first page of the book that is to be at the right end of the row.

Place the two books on your desk with the other books in between and your cardboard supports will hold the whole lot neatly in position. Now you can get on with that project in peace.

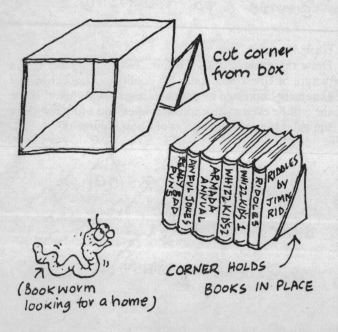

cut corner from box

(Bookworm looking for a home)

CORNER HOLDS BOOKS IN PLACE

Tidy Tie Tie

Do you have trouble every morning tying your school tie? It is a bit of a nuisance, isn't it? Well, adapt your tie to the Whizzkid's special method. You will have the neatest tied tie in the school, and you will never have to tie a tie ever again.

First you get an expert at tying ties to tie your tie for you. Now have someone cut through the tie at the back of your neck. (Do not ask Dracula to do this for you; his interest in your neck may not be confined to your tie!)

Ask your mother to sew the cut edges so they do not fray. At the same time get her to put a press stud on each of the cut ends.

Now all you have to do in the morning is to hold the tie around your neck and snap the two pieces together. Occasionally you may have to tighten the knot, but you won't have to tie your tie again—unless you change your school and the school tie is different.

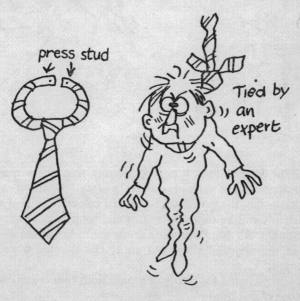

press stud

Tied by an expert

67

The Magic Pencil

Show your friends a pencil claiming that it has magical powers. "It can write any colour," you say. "Whatever colour you name, the pencil will write that colour." Some of your friends will be taken in by this and actually call out some colours. All you do is write down the names of the chosen colours saying, "There you are, I said it could write any colour!"

Be prepared for plenty of groans from your friends when you try this stunt.

It All Adds Up

Mathematics can be a most confusing subject, especially if you would rather be watching television instead of proving that x = y or something equally useless. But if mathematics is a subject that makes no sense to you, do not despair—you are not the only one in this predicament, as these examples prove.

Q.E.D. (Quite Easily Done)

A pupil watched a teacher writing the number 15.4 on the blackboard. As if the decimal point on its own was not confusing enough, the teacher went on to explain that to multiply the number by 10 all that is necessary is to move the decimal point one place to the right. To demonstrate this, the teacher then rubbed out the decimal point with a duster. Pointing to a poor unfortunate pupil who had done nothing wrong to deserve such attention, the teacher asked: "Where is the decimal point now?"

The pupil summoned up what little mental ability he had and gave the only answer he could think of: "It's on the duster, sir."

A similar problem was experienced by another pupil at another school. The teacher had asked: "If you found 20p in one pocket and 15p in the other pocket, what would you have?"

Not being a mathematical genius, there was only one suitable reply as far as the pupil was concerned: "I'd have someone else's trousers on."

I'd have someone else's trousers on

Elsie doesn't wear trousers

To make mathematical problems more interesting, many teachers try to relate them to everyday life. Sometimes this approach can lead to the teacher's downfall, as in the case of the one who said: "There are five people at a meal table but there are only four potatoes. How does the cook ensure that everyone gets a fair share?"

"Mash the potatoes," was the immediate reply.

The same thing happened to a teacher who posed this problem to a pupil: "If I gave you three mice today and four mice tomorrow, how many mice would you have?"

"Nine, sir," the pupil replied.

"Nine!" exclaimed the teacher.

"Yes, sir. I've got two mice already."

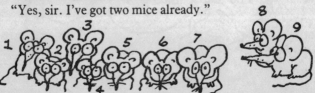

Another teacher once asked a pupil: "If your father borrows £12 from me and pays me back at £1 per month, how much will he owe me after five months?"

There was not a moment's hesitation as the pupil replied, "£12, sir."

"I'm afraid you don't know much about arithmetic," said the teacher.

"And I'm afraid you don't know much about my father," the pupil replied.

I'm afraid you don't know my father, sir...

TEACHER: What is two and two?
PUPIL: Four.
TEACHER: That's good.
PUPIL: Good! It's absolutely perfect.

TEACHER: What is five and three?
PUPIL: I don't know, sir.
TEACHER: You don't know! It's eight, of course.
PUPIL: But, sir! You told us yesterday that four and four is eight!

Arithmetic teachers have to be careful how they pose their problems if there is a Whizzkid in the class. One teacher asked a Whizzkid: "If eggs are 35p a dozen, how many would you get for 15p?"

To this problem the Whizzkid replied: "None, sir."

This perplexed the teacher a little. "None?" he queried.

"That's right, sir," replied the Whizzkid. "I'd buy a bar of chocolate instead."

After the last example, the teacher tried another tactic, but once again the Whizzkid was too quick for him. Leaving the eggs aside, the teacher asked: "Well, if you bought forty jam tarts for 25p, what would each one be?"

The reply was instantaneous: "They'd be stale."

Pen in the Pocket

Next time you have to borrow a pen from a friend, try this.

When you have finished using the pen pretend to put it in your side coat pocket. What you really do is drop the pen down your right sleeve. As it falls down the sleeve, catch it in your right hand. By this time your friend will be demanding his pen back. Reach into your right-hand pocket and apparently remove the pen from it. If you do this casually— and not too often—your friend will receive quite a shock. You placed the pen in one pocket and removed it from another!

your friend will receive quite a shock!

More From the Whizzkid's Library

Here are some more of the most popular books to be found in the Whizzkid's school library:

ON THE ROAD by Laurie Driver
SCHOOL SPORTS DAY by Arthur Lectics
THE POSTSCRIPT by Adeline Extra
AROUND THE MOUNTAIN by Sheila B. Cummin
NEVER GIVE UP by Percy Vere
LUNCH ON A DIET by Roland Butter
THE NAUGHTY SCHOOLBOY by Enid Abeatin
HOW TO INCREASE YOUR HEIGHT by U. R. Short
HAVE A SWEET by Arthur N. E. More
HOW TO REPAIR A CAR by Mick Anik
RUSH OVER THE RIVER by Bridget Cwik
ARE THEY YOURS? by Joan Emm
TIGER ATTACK by Claude Toobits

Tiger Attack
by Claude Toobits

Spelling Test

Can you say what each group of letters spells?

XPDNC   XLNC

NRG   AGNC

DK   XQQ

LEG   INXINXIN

Answers on page 128

Coin Column

Place about ten coins in a pile on a plate. Now challenge your friends to put the coins in a pile on the table. The coins must be in exactly the same order as they are on the plate, and no-one is allowed to touch them in any way. Some of your clever friends may try sliding the coins from the plate but their attempts will all end in failure. Eventually everyone will give up and then you can demonstrate how the problem is solved.

Hold the plate with the coins on it about 35 centimetres above the table. Quickly bring it down to within 10 centimetres of the table top and then sharply towards yourself. The coins will fall in a pile on the table, much to the amazement of your friends.

It is a good idea to practise this in private first as you may not be able to do it straight away. After a few attempts you should have gained the knack and the confidence to achieve success on every attempt.

You may not be able to do it right away.

Look in at Your Library

Not far from your house is a gateway to all knowledge — your local library. Contrary to popular opinion, a library is not a boring place, for on its shelves can be found a world of wonder into which you can delve at will. It is a place with which all Whizzkids should be familiar.

Using a public library is really quite simple. If you have not used one before, ask the librarian to show you the ropes. Or perhaps your teacher would be prepared to organise a trip. You will find that most libraries issue helpful leaflets and may have a floor plan on display to help you find your way around.

Ask the librarian to show you the ropes...

The books in most libraries are arranged in subject order according to the Dewey Decimal Classification System. This divides all knowledge into ten main subject groups as follows:

000	Generalities
100	Philosophy
200	Religion
300	Social Sciences
400	Language
500	Pure Sciences
600	Applied Sciences and Technology
700	The Arts
800	Literature
900	Geography and History

It is useful, but not essential, if you learn these. Each of the ten divisions is then futher subdivided into ten. Here is the complete list:

000	*Generalities*	100	*Philosophy*
010	Bibliographies and catalogues	110	Metaphysics
020	Library science	120	Metaphysics
030	General encyclopedias	130	Fields of psychology
040	Collected essays	140	Philosophical views
050	General periodicals	150	Psychology
060	Museums and societies	160	Logic
070	Journalism	170	Ethics
080	Collected works of authors	180	Ancient and oriental philosophy
090	Manuscripts and rare books	190	Modern philosophy

200	*Religion*	300	*Social Sciences*
210	Natural religion	310	Statistics
220	The Bible	320	Political science
230	Christian theology	330	Economics
240	Christian theology	340	Law
250	Christian theology	350	Public administration
260	Christian theology	360	Social welfare
270	History and geography of the Christian church	370	Education
280	Christian churches and sects	380	Commerce
290	Other religions and comparative religion	390	Customs and folklore

400	*Language*	500	*Pure Sciences*
410	Linguistics	510	Mathematics
420	English	520	Astronomy
430	German	530	Physics
440	French	540	Chemistry and mineralogy
450	Italian and Romanian	550	Earth sciences
460	Spanish and Portuguese	560	Paleontology
470	Latin	570	Biology
480	Greek	580	Botany
490	Other languages	590	Zoology

Zoology

Recreation

600	*Technology and Applied Science*	700	*The Arts and Recreation*
610	Medical sciences	710	Landscape architecture
620	Engineering	720	Architecture
630	Agriculture	730	Sculpture
640	Home economics	740	Drawing
650	Business	750	Painting
660	Chemical technology	760	Graphic arts
670	Manufacturing	770	Photography
680	Manufacturing	780	Music
690	Building	790	Recreation

800	*Literature*	900	*General Geography and History*
810	American	910	General geography
820	English	920	General biography
830	German	930	Ancient world history
840	French	940	European history
850	Italian and Romanian	950	Asian history
860	Spanish and Portuguese	960	African history
870	Latin	970	North American history
880	Greek	980	South American history
890	Literature of other languages	990	Other countries and other worlds

HOW!

North American History

These divisions are then further subdivided and each subject is in turn broken down into more specific subheadings, each of which is given a code number separated from the subject number by a decimal point. You do not have to know these code numbers, but you will find it well worthwhile remembering the complete number classification of any subjects in which you have a particular interest.

The books are filed in numerical order. This means that all the books on a particular subject can be found in one place and you do not have to wander around the library searching vainly for what you want. The classification number is usually written on the spine of each book.

Biographies and autobiographies (which are not biographies about cars!) are arranged alphabetically under the name of the person written about. Fiction is arranged in alphabetical order or the authors' surnames.

You are normally allowed to borrow up to four books at one time, but if you are doing a special project the librarian may be prepared to let you have more. All books must be

returned to the library from which they were borrowed. The date by which each book is to be returned is usually stamped on a card or a sheet inserted in the book. You are normally allowed to borrow each book for about three weeks but it is possible to have it reissued for a further period provided that no other readers are waiting for it.

If you require a book that you are unable to find on the shelves, ask the librarian if he or she can obtain it for you. You will be asked to fill in a card giving details of the book you want. This card will be posted to you when the book is available. Usually you will be asked to pay the postage for the card—a small price to pay for such a wonderful service.

One part of the library from which you cannot borrow books is the reference section. This contains dictionaries, encyclopedias, and so on. You are, however, allowed to refer to these books in the library. It is a good idea to take a good look at the reference section to see what books are available. You will find some of these books invaluable when working on projects.

Many other services are offered by your library, so ask your librarian about them. Librarians are always happy to answer any genuine queries. But please remember that they are busy people—do not waste their time with unnecessary questions.

Every Whizzkid worth his or her salt (or vinegar) makes full use of the library service. So look in at your local library and begin to find out about the wide range of information and pleasure that is available.

Double It

Can you think of anything from which you can take half and yet still end up with twice as much as you started with? That is the question you pose to a friend. But before reading any further, see if you can work it out.

Give up? All you have to do is to write on a piece of paper, "Half a pound". Show this to your friend. Now use the pencil to cross through the word "half" and you are left with "a pound". So you took away half from half a pound and ended up with a pound—twice as much as you started with!

Find the Inventors

Hidden in the grid of letters on the opposite page are the surnames of thirty-three famous inventors. They may be written forwards, backwards, up and down, or diagonally. The full names are listed below, and to please your teachers in the hope that you might learn something, some of their inventions are listed as well. See how many of the surnames you an find in the grid.

Richard ARKWRIGHT (spinning frame)
Alexander Graham BELL (telephone)
Lazlo BIRO (ballpoint pen)
Robert von BUNSEN (bunsen burner)
Christopher COCKERELL (hovercraft)
Samuel CROMPTON (spinning "mule")
Humphrey DAVY (miner's safety lamp)
James DEWAR (vacuum flask)
Rudolph DIESEL (diesel engine)
Thomas EDISON (electric light)
Michael FARADAY (dynamo)
Benjamin FRANKLIN (lightning conductor)
Galileo GALILEI (thermometer)
Henry GREATHEAD (lifeboat)
Johann GUTENBERG (moveable type)
James HARGREAVES (spinning jenny)
Elias HOWE (sewing machine)
John KAY (flying shuttle)
Hiram MAXIM (automatic gun)
Samuel MORSE (morse code)
William MURDOCK (coal gas lighting)
Alfred NOBEL (dynamite)
Charles PARSONS (steam turbine)
Blaise PASCAL (adding machine)
Louis PASTEUR (immunization)
Wilhelm ROENTGEN (x-ray tube)
Christopher L. SHOLES (typewriter)
William SYMINGTON (steamboat)

Evangeslista TORRICELLI (barometer)
L.E. WATERMAN (fountain pen)
James WATT (steam engine)
Frank WHITTLE (jet engine)
Ferdinand ZEPPELIN (rigid airship)

Answers on page 127

```
W  I  G  G  O  N  O  B  E  L  E  S  E  I  D
A  J  R  K  U  O  F  B  R  H  A  B  R  Z  O
T  O  E  O  P  T  G  R  G  A  L  I  L  E  I
T  T  A  W  A  P  E  M  A  R  A  S  L  P  T
W  A  T  E  R  M  A  N  J  G  R  Y  E  P  F
H  U  H  O  S  O  R  I  B  R  K  M  R  E  I
I  L  E  N  O  R  J  L  U  E  W  I  E  L  L
T  D  A  N  N  C  J  K  N  A  R  N  K  I  L
T  O  D  O  S  C  G  N  S  V  I  G  C  N  E
L  P  A  S  C  A  L  A  E  E  G  T  O  R  C
E  C  R  I  O  M  R  R  N  S  H  O  C  R  I
D  Y  A  D  A  R  A  F  R  Y  T  N  I  I  R
A  R  B  E  L  L  W  X  P  A  S  T  E  U  R
V  I  S  H  O  L  E  S  I  B  O  W  R  F  O
Y  A  K  K  C  O  D  R  U  M  O  R  S  E  T
R  O  E  N  T  G  E  N  J  H  M  O  F  D  R
```

Easy Exam

The trouble with most examinations is that the questions are too difficult to answer. But here, for the first time in history, is an exam that is so easy that anyone can get full marks. Or can they? Try to answer the following questions and you may find that his exam is not quite so easy as it may at first appear.

1. What type of animal is a panda bear?
2. What is the name of the famous man-made monster in a novel by Mary Shelley?
3. Which is heavier, a pint of hot water or a pint of cold water?
4. From what creature is cat gut obtained?
5. Where does Dresden china come from?
6. In which country did the Chinese dish chop suey originate?
7. Where did Turkish baths originate?
8. What type of creature is a firefly?
9. What type of creature is a horned toad?
10. How long was the hundred years war?

How long was the hundred years war?

11. What was the relationship of James I of England to James VI of Scotland?
12. Harry S. Truman was an American President. What did the S in his name stand for?
13. What happened in England on 8th September, 1752?
14. Where in 1066 did the Battle of Hastings take place?

15. What is rice paper made from?
16. In which country did Indian ink originate?
17. If the word "cinque" is derived from the French word *cinq* meaning "five", how many cinque ports are there in England?
18. In which country did the Chinese willow pattern used on pottery originate?
19. William Cody was given the nickname "Buffalo Bill" because he was believed to have killed more than 4,000 of a certain type of animal. What were the animals he killed?
20. After what creature are the Canary Islands named?
21. From what type of hair are camel hair brushes made?
22. In what country was the Jerusalem artichoke first cultivated?

Answers on page 128

The Dancing Teacher

You may often lead your teacher a merry dance, but now you can do it literally. With this device you can make your teacher dance at your command, whenever you wish!

First you must make a small cardboard replica of your teacher like the one shown in the illustration. It greatly adds to the fun if you make the limbs jointed. To do this you cut around each limb and then join the pieces together with wire, cotton, or paper fasteners.

When it is finished you show the teacher to your friends. You then stand it between the legs of a desk at the far end of the classroom and the figure begins to dance! After a short while you pick it up and again hand it around to your friends, but they will not be able to discover how the animation was accomplished.

No doubt you, too, are wondering how the dancing was achieved. It is really quite simple. Before showing the trick to anyone you secretly push a drawing pin into the back of each of two desk legs. A dark piece of cotton is attached to one of the pins and this pin is pushed right into the desk leg. The thread then goes over the other drawing pin (do not push this one right in) and then to a nearby chair.

When the time comes to show your amazing dancing teacher, a friend who is in the know sits in the chair and casually picks up the thread from the floor. You place the figure between the desk legs in such a way that its arms go over the cotton. When your accomplice pulls on the cotton, the teacher appears to dance. It is as simple as that!

One word of warning. Don't let the teacher concerned see your animated friend. If you do, it could be you, not the teacher, that does the most dancing!

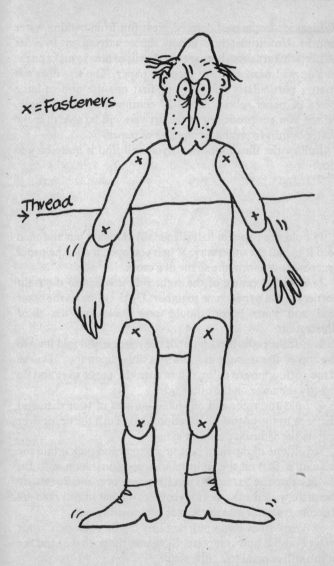

x = Fasteners

Thread →

Bombs Away!

Whizzkids in the past derived great fun from making water bombs. Unfortunately, it is now almost a dying art. In order to keep this art alive, here are the details of how to make one.

You will need a square piece of paper. The size does not matter particularly but for your first one use quite a large piece of paper, about 20 by 20 centimetres, for example. When you get proficient at the art you will be able to make water bombs from almost any size of paper.

Follow the illustrations and you will find it quite easy to do.

1. Fold the paper in half diagonally. Open it out and then fold it in half the other way. When you open it out, the paper creases should form the shape of a cross.

2. Fold the centre of the right side inwards so the right corners of the paper come together. Do the same on the other side and your paper should now look like the third illustration.

3. Lift the right-hand point of the triangle and fold it up to the top of the triangle as shown in illustration four. Do the same with opposite point. Then turn the paper over and do exactly the same on the other side.

4. Fold the right and left-hand corners of your diamond shape in to the centre (illustration five). Turn the paper over and do the same on the other side.

5. Lift one of the right bottom corners and tuck it into the triangular flap on the right-hand side (illustration six). Do the same on the left side. Turn the paper over and do exactly the same with the two bottom corners on that side. Try to get the corners as far into the flap as you possibly can.

6. Apart from some puff applied to the open part, your water bomb is now complete. Blow into the open part and the bomb will expand to a cube shape.

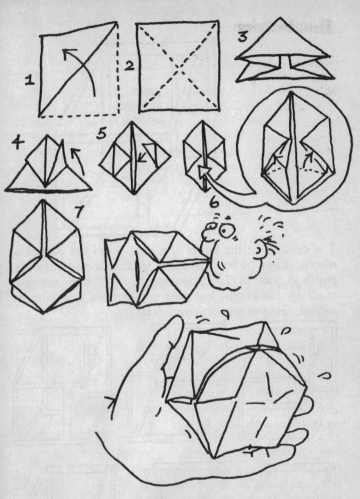

What, you may ask, is the purpose of this strange item and why is it called a water bomb? Well, in the past naughty children used to fill them with water and then throw them at their friends or drop them from an upstairs window on to their teachers. But you wouldn't do anything as dastardly as that, would you?

Plan Puzzler

IVOR PLANK'S WHOTSIT

The drawing at the top of this page shows the plan of a whotsit drawn by Ivor Plank, the woodwork master, for his pupils to make in class. Below are six copies of the drawing made by his pupils, but only one of them is absolutely correct. Can you spot which one it is?

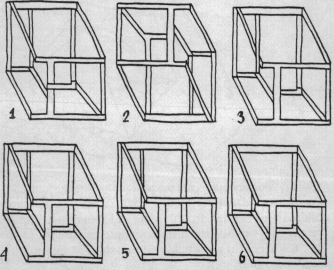

1

2

3

4

5

6

Answer on page 128

There's a Hole in the School Roof

On a rainy day you suddenly look up at the ceiling and exclaim: "The rain is coming in!" Your friends will think you are a bit of a drip because they cannot see any drips. To prove that you are telling the truth (oh, you are a fibber!), you hold a pencil and a sheet of paper as shown. Everyone will then be convinced you are truthful, or crazy, for they hear the drips of water hitting the paper!

There is no water, of course. The noise is actually made by holding the pencil and paper tightly in the position shown and pushing forward with your thumb. This causes the paper to move forward in small jerks. Each jerk produces a loud tap, but the movement of the paper is so slight that it cannot be seen.

You could also make use of this little stunt in the school dining room. Go around the room making the taps as you swat imaginary flies. That should please the school cook!

Desk Tidy

To keep all your pens and pencils tidy on your homework desk you will need this desk tidy. It is very easy to make.

Get the inners of three toilet or kitchen rolls. Cut each one to a slightly different length. You must now make bottoms for each of these tubes. To do this, place the tube on to a sheet of thin card. With a pencil draw around the tube. Now draw a slightly larger circle around the first and cut small "teeth" in it as shown in the illustration. If you bend these teeth up you can easily glue the round piece of card to the tube. Do the same with the other two tubes.

Now glue the three tubes together for the whole of their length and then glue them onto a piece of thick card which will act as the base. The tubes can now be stood on your desk as a handy place to put your pencils, sticks of dynamite and other essentials. The tubes can of course be decorated. The easiest way to do this is to stick coloured paper round them before they are glued together.

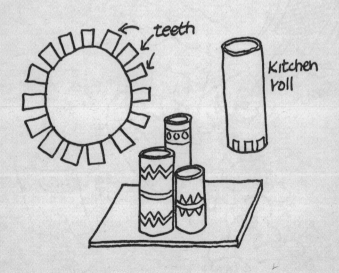

teeth

Kitchen roll

Why Fire Engines Are Red

The keen Whizzkid is always ready to amaze teachers, parents and friends with fantastic facts and bits of useless information. If anyone asks a Whizzkid why fire engines are red, this is the usual reply:

Fire engines have eight men and four wheels.
Eight and four make twelve.
Twelve inches equal one foot.
One foot is the length of a ruler.
Queen Elizabeth the First was a ruler.
Queen Elizabeth knighted Frances Drake.
Drake sailed the seven seas.
In the seas there are fish.
Fish have fins.
Fins live in Finland.
Finland is next to Russia.
The Russian flag is red.
AND THAT'S WHY FIRE ENGINES ARE RED!

Move It

Place a very small piece of paper on a table. The smaller the paper the better—about one centimetre square is sufficient. Now claim that you will make the paper move but you will not touch it, blow on it, touch the table, or touch the paper with anything. You further state that you will not ask anyone else to do any of these things but you will still cause the paper to move. As you appear to have mentioned every possibility, no-one will believe that you can make the paper move. But you do.

All you have to do is remove a comb from your pocket and run it through your hair a few times. Now hold the comb near the paper the static electricity you have created will cause the paper to move. This prank is not recommended for use by bald people.

Whizzkid's Dictionary

These daft definitions may make sense to a Whizzkid, but you will not find them in any ordinary dictionary.

ACCORD — a piece of string

ACORN — something caused by a tight shoe

ADDRESS — clothing worn by a girl

ADORE — the entrance to a house

ADVICE — something everybody gives but which few people take

ARCHEOLOGIST — a person whose career is in ruins

ARGUMENT — when two people are trying to get the last word in first

BARBER — a man who talks behind your back

BUOYANT — a male ant

BOYCOTT — a bed for a baby boy

BIRD CAGE — home tweet home

BUTTRESS — a female goat

CATERPILLAR — an upholstered worm

CHEDDAR GORGE — an enormous cheese sandwich

C.I.D. — Copper In Disguise

COCONUT — a person who is crazy about hot chocolate

COUGH — something you can't help but which everyone else does to annoy you

DIVINE — what de grapes grow on

DOGMA — the mother of pups

ECLIPSE — what a gardener does to a hedge

EMULATE — a dead emu

EPISTLE — the wife of an apostle

FATHER'S DAY — just like Mother's Day—but the present is smaller

FRIEND — someone who has the same enemies as you

GIRAFFE — the highest form of animal life

GLADIATOR — what a cannibal is after having a lady for lunch

GOOSE — a bird that grows down as it grows up

GOSSIP — a person who gives you the benefit of the dirt

HAIL — hard-boiled rain

ILLEGAL — a sick bird

LESSON — what you have when you remove some clothes

MINIMUM — a small mother

MORTAR BOARD — a hat used by teacher for mixing cement

MYTH — a female moth

NET — holes tied together with string

OUT OF BOUNDS — an exhausted kangaroo

PARROT — a wordy birdy

SKELETON — a person with his outsides off and his insides out

STREAKY BACON — a pig with no clothes on

TEACHER — a person who is always late for school when you are early and early when you are late

TEACHER — someone who talks in your sleep

TEMPER — something you can lose but still have

URCHIN — the lower part of a girl's face

VOLCANO — a mountain with hiccups

VOLGA BOATMAN — a rude sailor

YARD — something that has three feet but can't walk

ZEBRA — a horse with venetian blinds

ZOO — a place people visit but where animals are barred

School Days

It is often said (by grown-ups — not by kids) that school days are the happiest days of your life. That statement is open to debate, but school days can certainly be the funniest if the jokes on the following pages are anything to go by.

TEACHER: It is an established scientific fact that heat causes expansion and cold causes contraction. Who can give me an example?
PUPIL: I can, sir. In the summer when it's hot the days are longer than in the winter when it's cold.

FATHER: Why are your school marks always so low?
BOY: Because I sit at the back of the class.
FATHER: What difference does that make?
BOY: Well, there are lots of people sitting in front of me so that when it's my turn to receive marks there aren't many left.

FATHER: How was your first day at school?
BOY: Not too bad, but they forgot to give me my present.
FATHER: Present? What present?
BOY: Well, when I went into the classroom the teacher said, "You sit there for the present." Perhaps she will give it to me tomorrow.

When little Johnny brought home his school report, his father was less than pleased. As he read through the bad report his face went redder and redder as he became angrier and angrier. As last he could contain his anger no longer. "It says here that you came bottom in a class of twenty," he exploded. "That is disgraceful!"

"It could have been worse, Dad," said the boy. "There could have been more kids in the class."

FATHER: What did you learn at school today?
DAUGHTER: I learned that the sums you did for my homework were all wrong.

100

FATHER: Hold out your hand. I'm going to give you the cane.
PUPIL: Oh, thank you, sir. What shall I do with it?

The boys, fighting in the school playground, were pulled apart by a prefect. "You know the school rules," he said. "No fighting allowed."

At this the two boys protested, "But we weren't fighting aloud, we were fighting quietly."

TEACHER: Why have you got cotton wool in your ears?
PUPIL: Yesterday you said everything you told me went in one ear and out the other. I'm trying to stop it.

MOTHER: Did you learn anything at school today?
SON: Yes, how to get out of class by stuffing red ink up my nose.

TEACHER: If we breathe in oxygen during the day, what do we breathe in at night?
PUPIL: Nitrogen.

TEACHER: Now, class, what would you all like to do?
PUPILS: Go home.

TEACHER: I wish you'd pay a little attention
PUPIL: I'm paying as little as I can, sir.

TEACHER: Why were you off school yesterday?
PUPIL: I was sick.
TEACHER: Sick of what?
PUPIL: Sick of school.

TEACHER: Why are you standing on your head?
PUPIL: I'm turning things over in my mind.

TEACHER: What is the outer part of a tree called?
PUPIL: I don't know, sir.
TEACHER: Bark, boy, bark!
PUPIL: Woof, woof, woof.

Art and Craft

Tell one of your teachers that you have for sale a beautiful copper plaque bearing a portrait of the Queen sculptured in bas relief. All you want for this genuine work of art is just ten pence. When the teacher hands you the ten pence, you give him a two pence coin!

English Lesson

TEACHER: Can you give me a sentence with the word "fascinate" in it?
PUPIL: My little brother has a coat with nine buttons but he can only fasten eight.

TEACHER: ·Can you give me a sentence with the word "centimetre" in it?
PUPIL: My aunt came to visit us and I was sent to meet her.

TEACHER: What is the longest sentence you can think of?
PUPIL: Life imprisonment.

TEACHER: What's the difference between an English teacher and an English book?
PUPIL: You can shut the book up.

TEACHER: Can you give me a sentence with the word "gruesome" in it?
PUPIL: My mum wanted some lettuces so my dad grew some.

Fleas

Among all the poems you may learn in your English lessons it is almost certain that your teacher will not mention one of the shortest poems in the English language. The poem was written about fleas by Britain's most prolific poet, Anon. Whether this was Algernon Anon or his sister Sharon Anon has not been discovered. But here for your ed-u-cat-i-on-anon is the poem:

> Adam
> Had 'em

Here is another short poem on the same subject:

> Big fleas have little fleas
> Upon their backs to bite 'em,
> And little fleas have lesser fleas
> And so on ad infinitum.

More Artful Art

Here are some more strange drawings with which you can puzzle your art teacher. But first, can you work out what each picture represents?

1

2

3

4

5

6

Answers on page 128

Capital Quiz

Test your knowledge of geography with this quiz. In the left column are the names of various capital cities from around the world. The appropriate countries are in the right-hand column but they are not in the correct order. See if you can put each capital with the correct country. When you have done this quiz, try it on your geography teacher.

BUDAPEST	EGYPT
CANBERRA	ENGLAND
WELLINGTON	PERU
LONDON	CHINA
BUENOS AIRES	DENMARK
WASHINGTON	HUNGARY
PARIS	NORWAY
BRUSSELS	NETHERLANDS
CAIRO	FRANCE
WARSAW	BELGIUM
AMSTERDAM	NEW ZEALAND
OSLO	ARGENTINA
ROME	U.S.A.
COPENHAGEN	ITALY
PEKING	POLAND
LIMA	AUSTRALIA

Answers on page 128

How to Keep the School Idiot Happy

All you need to keep the school idiot happy for hours is a small square of paper. On one side of the paper write in block capitals:

PLEASE
TURN
OVER

Do exactly the same on the other side.

Hand the paper to your idiot friend and tell him to obey the instructions (assuming, of course, that he can read). He turns the paper over, reads the instruction, turns the paper over, reads the instruction, turns the paper over, reads the instruction . . . It will keep him amused for ages.

If you do not have a school idiot, try it on a teacher.

How to Keep the School Genius Happy

When you have got the school idiot working with the piece of paper just described, you can get the school genius occupied with this one. Once again, all you need is a square of paper.

On one side of the paper write:

> THE STATEMENT ON
> THE OTHER SIDE
> OF THIS PAPER
> IS FALSE

On the other side of the paper you write:

> THE STATEMENT ON
> THE OTHER SIDE
> OF THIS PAPER
> IS TRUE

Hand this to the school genius and he will reason that if the first statement is true, the second statement must be false. But if number two is false then number one must also be false. If, however, one is false, number two must therefore be true. And if two is true then one must be true—and the whole logical sequence starts over again. It should keep the school genius engrossed for ages.

Do not give this one to a teacher. The mental strain might cause his brains to explode!

SCHOOL GENIUS

More Facts to Bamboozle Teachers

Napoleon Bonaparte was frightened of cats.

Contrary to popular belief, moths do not eat holes in clothes. It is their larvae that cause the problem.

Two-thirds of the weight of the human body is water.

The Roman snail, the largest snail in Britain, has more than 21,000 teeth.

Sir Walter Raleigh's wife carried his head around with her in a red leather bag after his execution in 1618.

LADY RALEIGH'S SHOPPING BASKET

Hens that drink fizzy water lay eggs with harder shells.

The most common disease in the world is tooth decay. About fifty per cent of British people have lost their natural teeth by the time they are middle-aged.

All whales, dolphins, porpoises and sturgeon that become stranded on British shores must be offered to the monarch.

The Idiot Test

Tell a friend that you are going to give him the "idiot test". All you are going to do is to see if he can follow simple directions.

Hold both hands out in front of you with the thumbs raised and say, "All I want you to do is to raise two fingers." Nine times out of ten your friend will duplicate your action, whereupon you say, "Yes, you certainly are an idiot — those are your thumbs."

Groans from History

First there was the Ice Age, then the Stone Age. What came next?
The sausage.

Some English monarchs were Henry VII, Henry VIII, Edward VI and Mary. Who came after Mary?
The little lamb.

What was the first thing George II did on coming to the throne?
He sat down.

What did Sir Walter Raleigh say when he dropped his cloak before Queen Elizabeth I?
Step on it, kid.

What were the Poles doing in Russia in 1940?
Holding up the telephone wires.

Bottom of the Class

Are you the school dunce? If you are, try not to worry about it. A lot of people who were bottom of the class went on to become famous.

The only thing Winston Churchill, the great statesman, got right in one Latin exam was his name.

Alfred Lord Tennyson, who became Poet Laureate in 1850, did not start to speak until he was four.

Before Isaac Newton became a great scientist he was bottom of the lowest form in the grammar school he attended.

Thomas Edison patented over a thousand inventions but at school he was always bottom.

Godfrey Housefield was not thought very bright at school but in 1979 he became joint winner of the Nobel Prize for Medicine.

One of Britain's greatest engineers, James Watt, was described by his teachers as "dull and inept".

Ten-year-old Albert Einstein was told by a teacher, "You will never amount to very much," and yet he became one of the world's greatest scientists.

When Henry Ford, founder of the Ford Motor Company, left school he had only a basic ability in reading and writing.

The great artist, Pablo Picasso, could hardly read or write when he was ten.

How to Prove You Are a Mathematical Genius

If you want to convince your teachers and friends that you are a mathematical genius, all you have to do is construct a magic square.

"What," you may ask, "is a magic square?" Well, it is not someone prim and proper who does conjuring tricks! A magic square is a square of numbers in which the numbers all total the same in a variety of different ways. Let's take a look at a typical magic square so you will have a better idea of what it is all about.

```
 7   2  34   9
12  31   3   6
 1   8  10  33
32  11   5   4
```

If you examine the number square shown above, you will see that each horizontal row adds up to 52. Not only that, but each vertical column totals 52 and each corner-to-corner diagonal adds up to 52. The four corner numbers when added together also total 52!

You will also find that the four numbers in each of the corners and the four numbers in the centre, as indicated by the squares shown below, add up to 52.

```
 7   2  34   9
12  31   3   6
 1   8  10  33
32  11   5   4
```

If you take the two numbers in the centre of the top line (2 and 34) and add them to the two numbers in the centre of the bottom line (11 and 5), you get 52. The same thing happens if you add the two centre numbers of the outer left-hand column (12 and 1) to the two centre numbers of the outer right-hand column (6 and 33).

As if that was not enough, you will also find that the two diagonals 12 and 2 when added to the opposite diagonals 5 and 33 also total 52. The same is true of the diagonals 34 and 6 when added to the opposite diagonals 11 and 1.

But the remarkable properties of this amazing magic square are still not exhausted (although *you* may well be after all that!). Draw a rectangle around any block of nine numbers (there are four possibles, as shown below) and you will find that the corner numbers of each block add up to—yes, you've guessed it—52!

7	2	34	9
12	31	3	6
1	8	10	33
32	11	5	4

Now all of that (if you have read all the way through) may seem highly remarkable. But the really amazing thing is that as a Whizzkid you can construct a magic square that totals almost any number mentioned by your arithmetic teacher or friends. To do this there are only five points you have to learn and remember.

1. First you have to memorise the square of numbers shown below. You could have this written on a small piece of card to remind you, but the stunt is much more effective if you carry the secret in your head (there's plenty of room).

7	2	(+3)	9
12	(*)	3	6
1	8	10	(+2)
(+1)	11	5	4

It looks a little complicated but it doesn't take very long to memorise.

It doesn't take very long to memorise....

2. You have to restrict the selected total to any number between 34 and 100.

3. You have to mentally deduct 21 from the selected number. The easiest way to do this in your head is to take away 20 and then deduct 1 from your answer.

4. You now have to write down the square of numbers as shown above, but in the square marked (*) you put the selected number minus 21. In the square indicated by (+1) you put the same number plus 1. (Thus, if the selected number for the total was 87 you would write 67 in this square—87–21+1)

In the square marked (+2) you put the first number (87–21) plus 2 and you add 3 to the first number for the square marked (+3). So, if the selected number was 78, the numbers you would put in the bracketed squares would be 57 (78–21), 58 (57+1), 59 (57+2), and 60 (57+3).

As a final example, take a look at this magic square for the number 94.

7	2	76	9
12	73	3	6
1	8	10	75
74	11	5	4

With a little practice it is possible to write down a magic square for any number between 34 and 100 very quickly indeed. What the people watching do not realise is that you already have three quarters of the square committed to memory and that all you have to calculate are the four missing numbers. In spite of the fact that this is fairly easy to do, you will find that this feat will soon gain you the reputation of being a mathematical genius.

A Hole in One

Show your teacher a sheet of paper. In the centre of the paper is a very small hole. You point out the hole and the fact that it is very small. Then you challenge him to push his finger through the centre of the paper without tearing it. He will have to give up, for it is absolutely impossible—unless you cheat.

All you have to do is to roll the paper up into a tube. Now push your finger into the cylinder you have formed—it is going through the centre just as you said!

English Test

Here are a few problems to test your knowledge of English.

Sentence of Noughts
Write down ten noughts and the word "trick" like this:

0 0 0 0 0 0 0 0 0 0 trick

Can you now add just six straight lines in such a way that a comprehensible sentence is formed?

What Day is It?
When the day after tomorrow is yesterday, today will be the same number of days from Sunday as today was from Sunday when the day before yesterday was tomorrow. What day is it today?

Senseless Sentence
Can you work out what this says?
　　Major BBBB marched his CCCC through
　　a field of pot00000000.

Spelling Test
What word is never spelt correctly?

Can You Read This?
Can you work out what this says?
    00,I00. DOU00?
    NOIDOOOO, IO 101p.

Words in a Word
Can you think of a word of seven letters in which the first two letters refer to a man, the first three letters refer to a woman, the first four letters make a brave man, and all seven letters are a brave woman?

Answers on page 128

Chain Male

On a piece of fairly stiff white card draw the head of your headmaster. Leave out the nose and mouth so it looks something like the one shown on this page. Make a small hole through the card at the top of the nose. Make another small hole at the bottom of the mouth. These positions are marked X in our drawing.

You will now need to buy a short length of fine black chain from your local hardware shop. By pushing a piece of fuse wire or a bent paperclip through the chain and the card and bending the wire at the back of the card you can fix the chain in position.

Hold the card and give it a shake. Each time you do this your headmaster's nose and expression changes as the chain adopts a new position. Do not let your headmaster see this or his real expression might change. If he is very strict, you could end up working on a chain gang!

Chain

Slick Lace-Up

A Whizzkid can look very smart—when he or she wants to!
But usually this smartness is achieved in a cunning way. No
Whizzkid likes to be bothered with a shoelace coming
undone, for example, so a Whizzkid method of tying shoe-
laces has been devised.

Cut the metal tab off one end of the lace. Tie a knot in that
end of the lace and then flatten the knot with a hammer. Be
careful that you don't flatten your fingers at the same time.
Thread the lace through one of the top eyelets of your shoe.
This should be done from underneath so the knot is then
concealed.

Now push the lace through the opposite eyelet from above.
Continue the lacing downwards until you reach the last hole.
Thread the lace from above and down through this last hole.
Now pass the lace up along the tongue (the shoe's tongue, not
yours!) and out at the top of the shoe.

Put the shoe on—the lace has to be left fairly loose to allow
you to do this—and then pull the top end of the lace until all
the loops are tight. Cut the free end of the lace so only a length
of about 21 centimetres hangs from the shoe. Tuck this into
the shoe and your slick lace up is complete. This method of
lacing shoes is a little different from the usual, but it looks
extremely neat—and you will never have to put up with a
bow coming undone ever again!

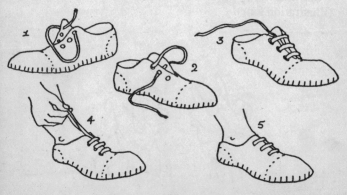

In a Tangle

For this neat little item you will need two pieces of soft string or rope, each about one metre long. You invite two friends to participate in a little puzzle.

Tie one end of the first piece of rope around the right wrist of the first person. The other end of the rope is tied around his left wrist. With the second piece of rope you tie up the second person in the same manner—but before tying the last wrist, you link the two ropes together as shown in the first illustration.

Now challenge your two friends (if they still are your friends) to separate themselves without cutting either of the ropes and without untying any of the knots. You will have great fun watching their antics as they try to separate the two ropes and it is very unlikely that they will discover the simple method by which this can be done.

After a while you will have to show them how. All you do is take the middle of the first person's rope. Push it through the loop around the right wrist of the second person. In doing this make sure that you push it through from the rear as shown in the second illustration.

Now slip the second person's right hand through the loop in the first person's rope (illustration three). Pull this loop back out through the rope around the second person's right wrist and you will find they are now both separated (illustration four).

124

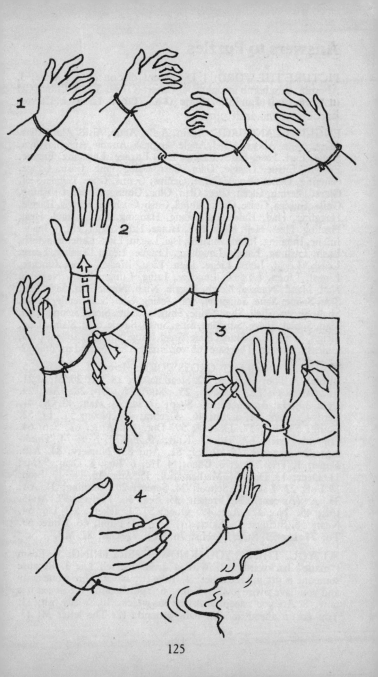

Answers to Puzzles

PICTURE THE WORD: 1. Discontent (disc on tent); 2. Hate; 3. Abominate (a bomb in eight); 4. Covert (C over T); 5. China (CH in A); 6. Finis (F in IS); 7. Ohio (O-high O); 8. Lacrosse (L across E).

ENGLISH LANGUAGE: Again, Agile, Ague, Aisle, Alas, Alias, Alien, Align, Allege, Angel, Angle, Anguish, Annual, Annul, Ashen, Eagle, Earl, Ease, Easel, Easing, Else, Engage, Engaging, Engine, Ensign, Ensue, Gaggle, Gain, Gala, Gale, Gang, Gash, Gauge, Gauging, Gene, Genial, Genie, Genius, Genus, Ghee, Giggle, Gill, Glare, Glaring, Glean, Glee, Glen, Glue, Gluing, Gnash, Gnashing, Guile, Guinea, Guise, Gull, Gunnel, Gush, Gushing, Haggis, Haggle, Haggling, Hail, Hale, Hall, Hang, Hanging, Hash, Haul, Heal, Healing, Heel, Hell, High, Hill, Hinge, Huge, Hull, Hung, Inane, Inhale, Inhaling, Insane, Insulin, Isle, Lagan, Lain, Lane, Languish, Lash, Lashing, Laugh, Laughing, League, Lean, Leaning, Lease, Leash, Legal, Lens, Liege, Lien, Lieu, Linage, Line, Lineage, Lineal, Linen, Lingual, Luggage, Lung, Lunge, Lush, Nagging, Nail, Nasal, Nausea, Neigh, Niggle, Nigh, Nine, Saga, Sage, Sail, Sale, Saline, Sane, Sanguine, Seal, Seeing, Seel, Sell, Senile, Senna, Shall, Sheen, Shell, Shin, Shine, Shingle, Shun, Siege, Sienna, Sigh, Sign, Signal, Silage, Sill, Sine, Sing, Singe, Single, Slag, Slain, Slang, Sleigh, Sling, Slug, Slung, Snag, Snail, Snug, Snuggle, Sullen, Ulna, Unleash, Unseen. There are 166 words here. Did you find any others?

WHIZZKID'S GIANT CROSSWORD: *Across:* 1. Teacher; 5. Rubik; 7. The; 10. Idea; 12. Headmaster; 18. Of; 20. Mead; 21. At (At-tack); 22. Lessons; 25. Star; 27. Op; 28. Arc; 29. Urn; 30. Ha; 32. Snake; 35. Soap; 37. Is; 38. Man; 40. Or; 41. Leo; 42. Rio; 44. Latin; 46. Algebra; 48. Noon; 51. Fi; 52. Going; 55. BC; 57. Essence; 59. Doh; 60. Attic; 62. Sap; 64. Cor; 65. Trick; 67. Tu; 68. Knit; 70. Pi; 72. Nor; 74. Thinking; 78. Rag; 79. If; 80. El; 81. Am; 83. Nursery; 84. Asp. *Down:* 1. Tri; 2. Ate; 3. Chaos; 4. He; 6. Bus; 8. Dam; 9. Mr; 11. Deer; 13. Des; 14. Mathematics; 15. Ada; 16. Ta; 17. Eton; 19 Foe; 22. Lab; 23. School; 24. Senior; 26. Running; 31. AA; 33. As (As-cent); 34. French; 35. Sea; 36. Prefect; 39. At; 43. Ibis; 45. No; 47. Age; 49. Oboe; 50. Crackers; 53. On; 54. Neat; 56. Strings; 58. Skirt; 61. Ton; 63. Pupil; 66. Knife; 69. To; 71. In; 73. Run; 74. His; 76. Key; 77. Gas; 82. MP.

SO YOU THINK YOU KNOW EVERYTHING: 1. Edam ("made" backwards); 2. With a druid-yourself kit; 3. Because someone is pulling the ropes; 4. Take two wires. Throw one away and you have a wire less; 5. None; 6. Your breath; 7. Same as it is now; 8. Are you asleep? 9. A nervous wreck; 10. A jelly fish; 11. You go on ahead and I'll hang around; 12. The letter M; 13.

Because it is in the middle of waTer; 14. Nuclear fission chips; 15. Olé (oh lay); 16. A centipede with a wooden leg; 17. Goldfish usually; 18. Have you ever tried ironing one? 19. It churns its own butter; 20. Because he had his work done by Friday; 21. A length of white cotton; 22. A length of white cotton with sunburn; 23. The shadow of the length of white cotton; 24. Chips that pass in the night; 25. William the Corn-curer.

ARTFUL ART: 1. Nothing on Earth; 2. Woman washing the floor; 3. A rough sea (a rough C); 4. Forked lightning; 5. A tap dancer; 6. Apple crumble.

CHANGING-ROOM CHANGES: Movement of hand of top left-hand player; spots on face of top left-hand player; tongue of bottom left-hand player; spot on player's chin; button on shirt of player holding the ball; creases on sock of player holding the ball; loss of a stripe on player's shirt; buttons on shirt of tall player; lace on boot of bottom right-hand player; the hair of Whizzkid peering in at top right-hand corner.

ARITHMETIC EXAM: $888+88+8+8+8=1,000$; 2. The number you should have written down is 12,111. If you write it bit by bit, you will see why: Eleven thousand (11,000) + Eleven hundred (1,100) + Eleven (11) = 12,111; 3. The postcard costs 2½p and the stamp is 22½p; 4. They weigh the same—one pound; 5. Six dozen dozen is 864 whereas half a dozen dozen is only 72—so six dozen dozen is the greater; 6. 42 kilograms; 7. Put 1 at the beginning of the number and 7 at the end to produce the answer, which is 116, 393, 442, 622, 950, 819, 672, 131, 147, 540, 983, 606, 557, 377, 049, 180, 327, 877.

RIVER ARRANGEMENT:

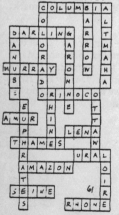

FIND THE INVENTORS:

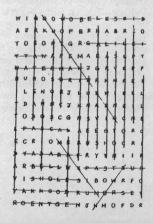

127

SPELLING TEST: PDNC = expediency; NRG = energy; DK = decay; LEG = elegy; XLNC = excellency; AGNC = Aegean Sea; XQQ = excuse (X Qs); INXINXIN = ink sinks in.

EASY EXAM: 1. A racoon; 2. Dr. Frankenstein's monster is not named; 3. Hot water is heavier than cold; 4. Sheep; 5. Meissen; 6. America; 7. Rome; 8. A beetle; 9. A lizard; 10. 116 years (1337 - 1453); 11. They were the same man; 12. The S had no meaning; 13. Nothing. On 2nd September, 1752 the English calendar was changed and the date was immediately altered to 14th September. The period between the two dates therefore never existed; 14. Not at Hastings but at Senlac Hill six miles away; 15. The pith of a tree; 16. China; 17. Fourteen. Dover, Sandwich, Hastings, Romney, Hythe, Rye, Winchelsea, Faversham, Folkestone, Lydd, Ramsgate, Margate, Deal, Tenterden; 18. In England about 1780; 19. Bison (there aren't any buffaloes in America); 20. "Dogs": the islands were named *Insulae Canariae* by the Romans and this means "Islands of Dogs"; 21. The tail hairs of squirrels; 22. Italy.

PLAN PUZZLER: Number 4 is correct.

MORE ARTFUL ART: 1. Worm climbing a razor blade; 2. Two Mexicans on a tandem; 3. A mink stole; 4. Man wearing a bow tie caught in lift doors; 5. Umbrella for a giraffe; 6. A camel passing the pyramids.

CAPITAL QUIZ: Budapest—Hungary; Canberra—Australia; Wellington—New Zealand; London—England; Buenos Aires—Argentina; Washington—U.S.A.; Paris—France; Brussels—Belgium; Cairo—Egypt; Warsaw—Poland; Amsterdam—Netherlands; Oslo—Norway; Rome—Italy; Copenhagen—Denmark; Peking—China; Lima—Peru.

ENGLISH TEST: *Sentence of Noughts*. The sentence is "good dog do a trick"; *What Day is It?* Sunday; *Senseless Sentence.* Major Forbes (four Bs) marched his forces (four Cs) through a field of potatoes (pot eight Os); *Spelling Test.* Incorrectly; *Can You Read This?* Owe nothing, I owe nothing. do you owe nothing? No I do not (nought) owe nothing, I owe over a pound; *Words in a Word.* Heroine (He, her, hero, heroine).